20/20
A CHRISTMAS COLLECTION

*Twenty Great Songs
Your Choir Can Learn
in Twenty Minutes!*

*With suggested Scriptures and service orders for
Christmas worship concert, Advent, and Christmas Eve by Lorie Marsh.*

Compiled by
DON MARSH

Arranged by
DENNIS ALLEN, KEITH CHRISTOPHER, TOM FETTKE,
BRUCE GREER, MARTY HAMBY, RICHARD KINGSMORE,
CAMP KIRKLAND, DON MARSH, DAVID McKAY, GARY RHODES

PRODUCTS AVAILABLE

Choral Book	0-6331-9499-9
Listening CD*	0-6331-9495-6
Accompaniment CD *(split track)*	0-6331-9528-6
Orchestration *(for all 20 songs)*	0-6331-9490-5
CD Promo Pak	0-6331-9493-X

*Listening CDs are available at a reduced rate when bought in quantities of 10 or more.

All orchestrations have been extracted from previous Genevox publications and may be ordered individually. "How Great Our Joy," "Like Christmas All Year 'Round," and "O Magnify" orchestrations have been appropriately modified to match the arrangements as they appear in 20/20: A Christmas Collection. Instrumentation may vary from piece to piece. Most include parts for all standard church orchestra instruments. Listening to the demonstration recording can provide a better idea of the instrumentation for each piece.

GENEVOX

0-6331-9499-9

© Copyright 2004 GENEVOX, Nashville, TN 37234. Possession of a CCLI license does not grant you permission to make copies of this piece of music.
For clarification about the rights CCLI grants you, please call 1-800-234-2446. Printed in the United States of America.

FOREWORD

Finding great songs and arrangements to sing at Christmas is a big task. The staff of Genevox and I hope that *20/20: A Christmas Collection* will make this task easier for you. These songs and arrangements, by some of today's most popular arrangers—Dennis Allen, Keith Christopher, Tom Fettke, Bruce Greer, Marty Hamby, Richard Kingsmore, Camp Kirkland, Don Marsh, David McKay, and Gary Rhodes—were chosen from LifeWay's vast music library.

This collection includes a good balance of popular carols, contemporary Christmas songs, and other specialty pieces. The arrangements and piano accompaniments were simplified to make them accessible to more choirs, but the "fun" and "sizzle" were left in. Wherever possible, choruses are voiced identically, so parts only have to be learned once. More unison voicing, two-part voicing, and optional solos were created to enable the choir to learn the arrangements in 20 minutes. (Please don't hold me to the 20 minutes, but I believe that most choirs can learn these arrangements in this time period.)

Lorie Marsh wrote suggestions for using these arrangements for a Christmas concert, to celebrate Advent, and as part of a Christmas Eve service. I pray that these suggestions will give you a head start as you prepare for the most beautiful season of music—Christmas.

I believe that you will find just about everything needed to create a joyous and meaningful Christmas season in *20/20: A Christmas Collection*. Go ahead, dig in!

Don Marsh

CONTENTS

Angels We Have Heard on High 92
    with Angels, from the Realms of Glory

Because of Bethlehem 151

Born in Bethlehem: A Medley of Christmas Spirituals 106
    includes Mary's Little Boy-Child (Because of Christmas
    Day)/Amen/The Virgin Mary Had a Baby Boy/Go, Tell It
    on the Mountain/Children, Go Where I Send Thee

Christmastime 5

Come, Let Us Go unto Bethlehem 77

Come to My Heart, Lord Jesus 118
    with Away in a Manger

From the Cradle to the Cross 59

God Rest Ye Merry, Gentlemen 23

Hark! The Herald Angels Sing 50

How Great Our Joy 176

I Wonder as I Wander 68

Jingle Bells Medley 128
    with Jingle Bells/Deck the Halls/O Christmas Tree/
    Here We Come A-Caroling

Joy to the World! The Lord Is Come 15
    with Joyful, Joyful, We Adore Thee

Light of the World 182

Like Christmas All Year 'Round 165

O Come, All Ye Faithful 160

O Magnify 140

Once and for All 98

Sing a Song of Christmas 194
    with Good Christian Men, Rejoice/Go, Tell It
    on the Mountain/Let Your Gladness Know No End

Sing Noel 32

Scriptures and Service Orders 205

Christmastime

Words and Music by
MICHAEL W. SMITH and
JOANNA CARLSON
Arranged by Bruce Greer
Adapted by Don Marsh

© Copyright 1998 and this arrangement © 2004 Sony/ATV Tunes LLC/
Deer Valley Music (both admin. by Sony/ATV Music Publishing, 8 Music Square West, Nashville, TN 37203)/
Lil' Yella House Music (admin. by Dayspring Music, LLC)/Dayspring Music, LLC.
All rights reserved. Used by permission.

Joy to the World! The Lord Is Come
with
Joyful, Joyful, We Adore Thee

ISAAC WATTS

GEORGE FREDERICK HANDEL
Arranged by Gary Rhodes
Adapted by Don Marsh

Arrangement © copyright 2002 Van Ness Press, Inc. (ASCAP). All rights reserved.

†"Joyful, Joyful, We Adore Thee." New words by NANCY GORDON and JOHN CHISUM. Music by LUDWIG van BEETHOVEN. © Copyright 2000 Integrity's Hosanna! Music (ASCAP)/Van Ness Press, Inc. (ASCAP)/Mother's Heart Music (ASCAP) (adm. by ROM Administration, P. O. Box 1252, Fairhope, AL 36532). All rights reserved. Used by permission.

Joy to the World! The Lord Is Come — 4

Joy to the World! The Lord Is Come — 8

God Rest Ye Merry, Gentlemen

†"God Rest Ye Merry, Gentlemen." Additional lyrics by NAN ALLEN. © Copyright 1998 Van Ness Press, Inc. (ASCAP) All rights reserved.

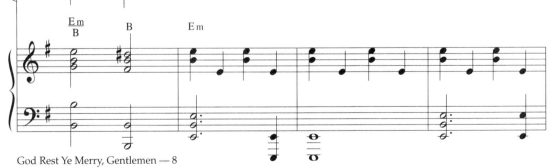

Sing Noel

Words and Music by
EDDIE CARSWELL and
MICHAEL O'BRIEN
Arranged by Bruce Greer
Adapted by Don Marsh

*Children's voices not included on split tracks. Throughout, children's choir part may be omitted or sung by select voices.

© Copyright 2001 and this arrangement © copyright 2003 Bridge Building Music/Sheltering Tree Music (BMI) (admin. by Brentwood-Benson Music Publishing, Inc.)/Designer Music Co. (SESAC) (admin. by BMG Music Publishing, Inc.). All rights reserved. Used by permission.

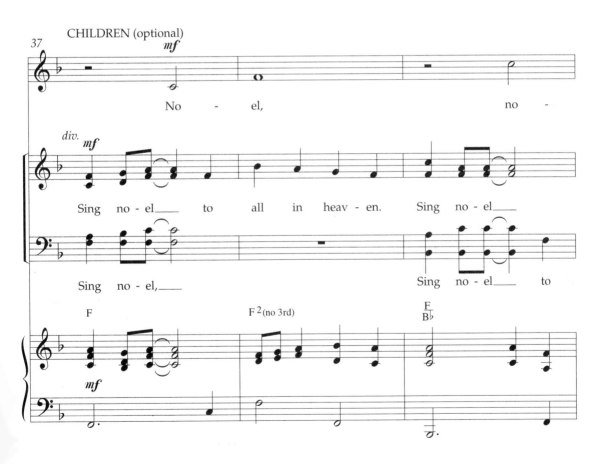

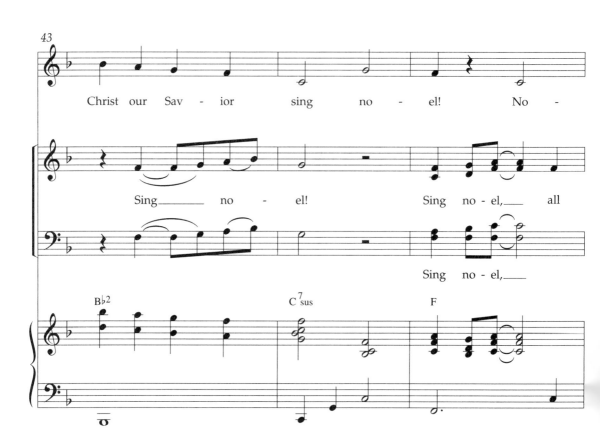

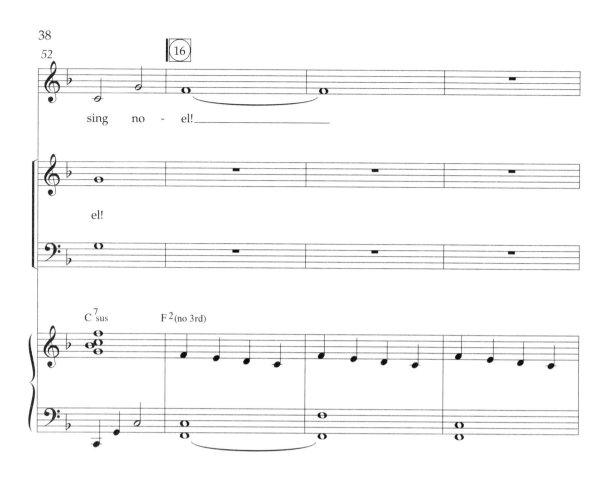

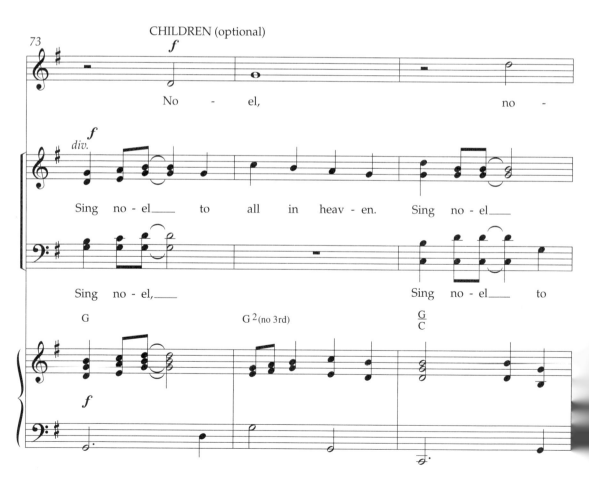

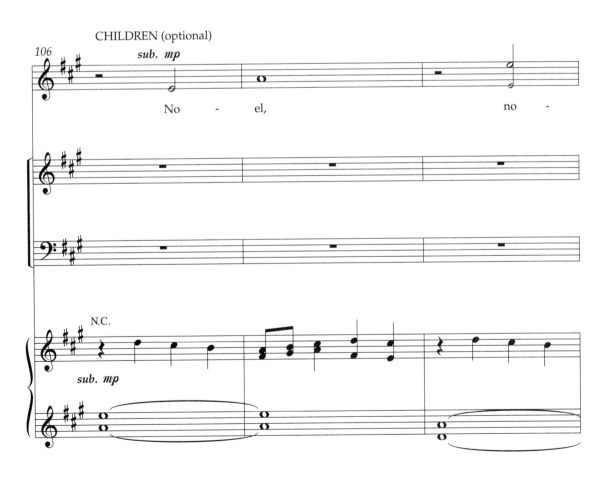

Hark! The Herald Angels Sing

CHARLES WESLEY
Altered by George Whitefield

FELIX MENDELSSOHN
Arranged by Richard Kingsmore
Adapted by Don Marsh

Hark! The Herald Angels Sing — 2

Hark! The Herald Angels Sing — 5

From the Cradle to the Cross — 3

From the Cradle to the Cross — 5

From the Cradle to the Cross — 9

I Wonder as I Wander

Traditional Appalachian Carol

JOHN JACOB NILES
Arranged by David McKay
Adapted by Don Marsh

Arr. © copyright 2002 McKinney Music, Inc. (BMI). All rights reserved.

Come, Let Us Go unto Bethlehem

KEITH FERGUSON

BRUCE GREER
Arranged by Bruce Greer
Adapted by Don Marsh

© Copyright 1999 Van Ness Press, Inc. (ASCAP). All rights reserved.

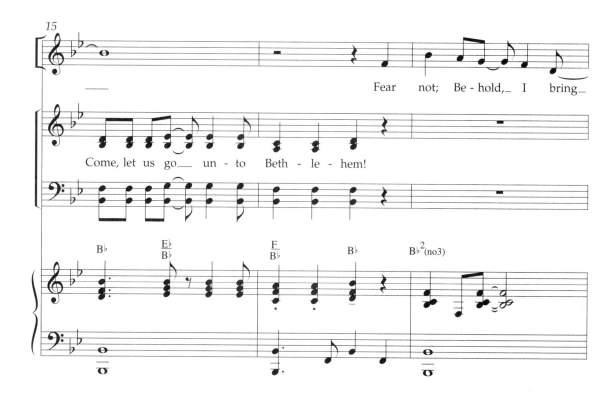

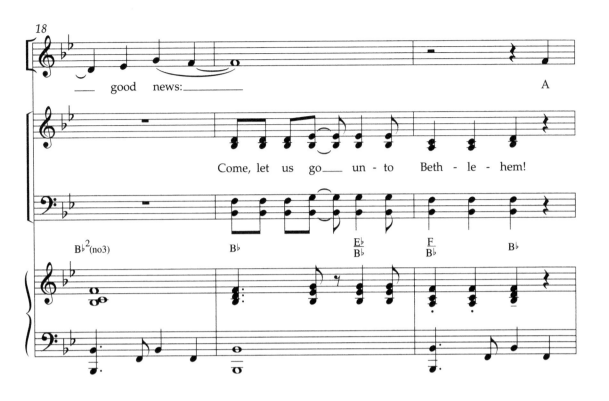
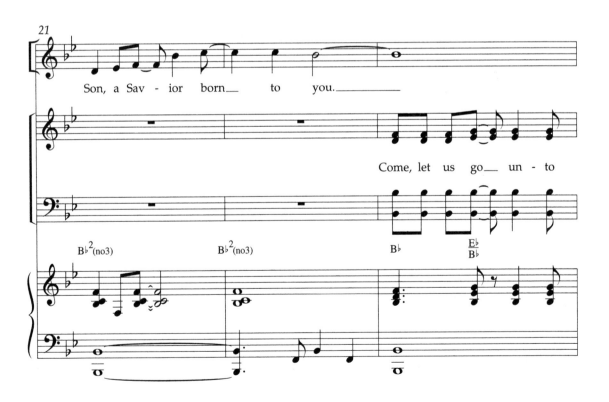

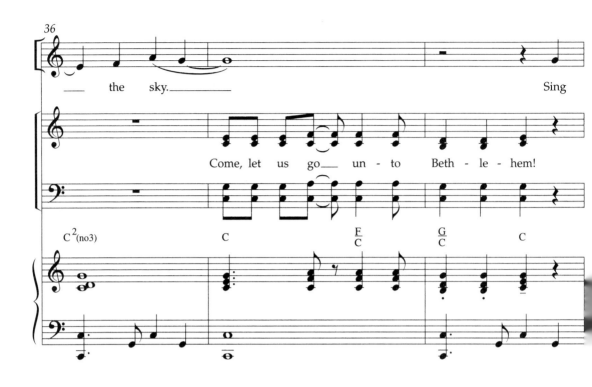

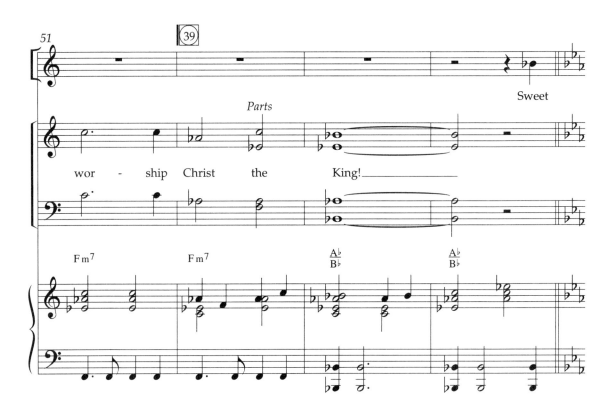

Angels We Have Heard on High
with
Angels, from the Realms of Glory

Traditional French Carol
Arranged by Tom Fettke
Adapted by Don Marsh

†"Angels We Have Heard on High." Traditional French Carol.

Arrangement © copyright 1997 Van Ness Press, Inc. (ASCAP).
All rights reserved.

†"Angels, from the Realms of Glory." Words by JAMES MONTGOMERY. Music by HENRY T. SMART.
Arr. © copyright 1997 Van Ness Press, Inc. (ASCAP). All rights reserved.

Once and for All

Words and Music by
JEFF SLAUGHTER and LORIE MARSH
Arranged and adapted by Don Marsh

© Copyright 1999 Van Ness Press, Inc. (ASCAP). All rights reserved.

Once and for All — 8

Born in Bethlehem
A Medley of Christmas Spirituals

Arranged by Bruce Greer
Adapted by Don Marsh

†"Mary's Little Boy-Child (Because of Christmas Day)." Words and music by JESTER HAIRSTON.

Arrangement © copyright 1999 Van Ness Press, Inc. (ASCAP). All rights reserved.

Born in Bethlehem — 2

†"Amen." Traditional.
††"The Virgin Mary Had a Baby Boy." Traditional.

Born in Bethlehem — 5

Born in Bethlehem — 8

†"Go, Tell It on the Mountain." Words by JOHN W. WORK, JR. Music African-American Spiritual.

Come to My Heart, Lord Jesus
with
Away in a Manger

EMILY E. S. ELLIOTT, adapted

TIMOTHY R. MATHEWS
Arranged by Keith Christopher
Adapted by Don Marsh

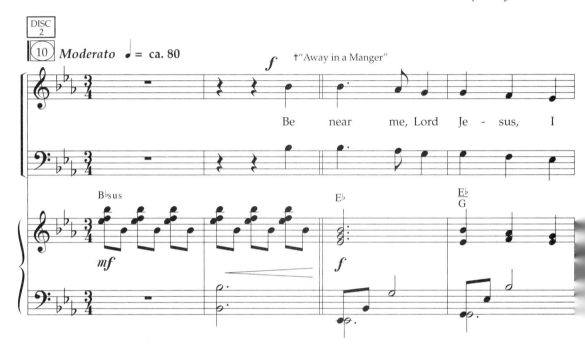

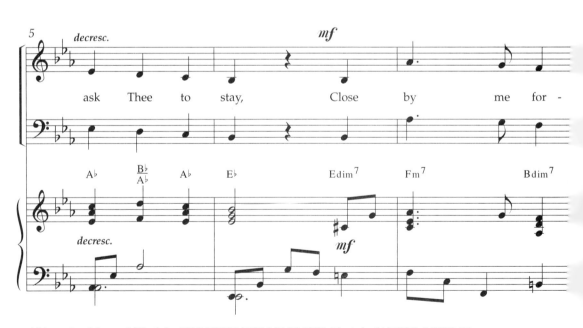

†"Away in a Manger." Words by JOHN THOMAS McFARLAND. Music by JAMES R. MURRAY.

Arrangement © copyright 2000 Van Ness Press, Inc. (ASCAP).
All rights reserved.

Come to My Heart, Lord Jesus — 3

Come to My Heart, Lord Jesus — 6

Jingle Bells Medley

includes
Jingle Bells
Deck the Halls
O Christmas Tree
Here We Come A-Caroling

Arranged and adapted by Don Marsh

† "Jingle Bells." Words and Music by JAMES PIERPONT.

Arrangement © copyright 2001 Van Ness Press, Inc. (ASCAP).
All rights reserved.

†"Deck the Halls." Words by J. P. McCASKEY. Music Ancient Welsh Melody.

Jingle Bells Medley — 7

†"O Christmas Tree." Words August Zarnack, *Weisenbuch zuden Volksliedern fur Volksschulen.*
Music Traditional German Carol.

†"Here We Come A-Caroling." Traditional English Carol.

Jingle Bells Medley — 10

O Magnify — 2

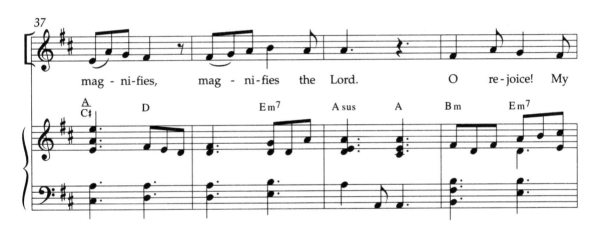

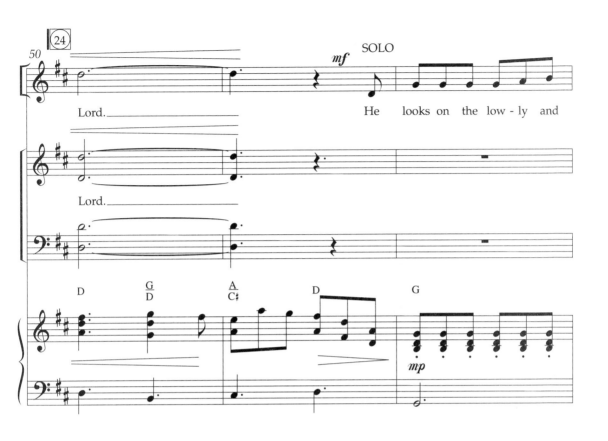

O Magnify — 8

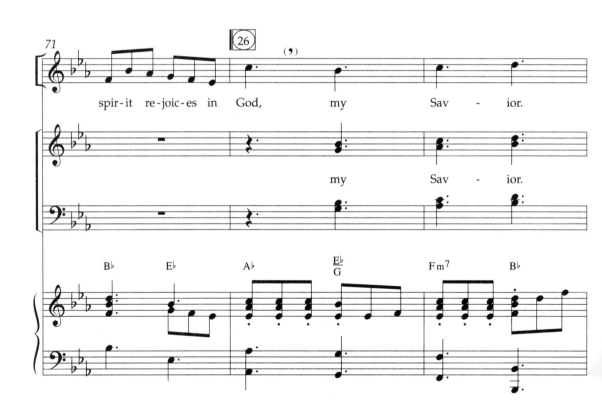

Because of Bethlehem — 5

156

†"O Little Town of Bethlehem." Words by PHILLIPS BROOKS. Music by LEWIS H. REDNER.

O Come, All Ye Faithful

Latin Hymn
Ascribed to John Francis Wade
Translated by Frederick Oakeley

JOHN FRANCIS WADE
Arranged by Tom Fettke
Adapted by Don Marsh

Arrangement © copyright 1997 Van Ness Press, Inc. (ASCAP). All rights reserved.

Like Christmas All Year 'Round

Words and Music by
DENNIS JERNIGAN
Arranged by Marty Hamby
Adapted by Don Marsh

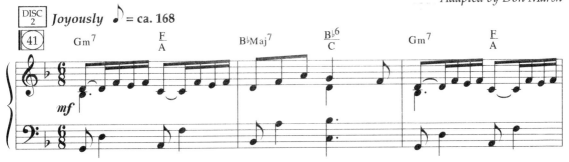

© Copyright 1992 and this arrangement © copyright 2000 Shepherd's Heart Music, Inc.
(admin. by Dayspring Music, LLC).
All rights reserved. Used by permission.

Like Christmas All Year 'Round — 2

Like Christmas All Year 'Round — 6

Like Christmas All Year 'Round — 9

Like Christmas All Year 'Round — 10

How Great Our Joy

Traditional German Carol

Traditional German Melody
Arranged by Tom Fettke
Adapted by Don Marsh

Arrangement © copyright 1997 Van Ness Press, Inc. (ASCAP). All rights reserved.

How Great Our Joy — 2

How Great Our Joy — 3

Light of the World

Words and Music by
DENNIS L. JERNIGAN
Arranged by Richard Kingsmore
Adapted by Don Marsh

© Copyright 1994 and this arrangement © copyright 2001 Shepherd's Heart Music, Inc.
(admin. by Dayspring Music, LLC).
All rights reserved. Used by permission.

Light of the World — 9

†"O Come, All Ye Faithful." Words Latin Hymn; ascribed to John Francis Wade; translated by Frederick Oakeley. Music by JOHN FRANCIS WADE.

Light of the World — 11

Sing a Song of Christmas

with
Good Christian Men, Rejoice
Go, Tell It on the Mountain
Let Your Gladness Know No End

Words and Music by
DON and LORIE MARSH
Arranged and adapted by Don Marsh

© Copyright 1999 Van Ness Press, Inc. (ASCAP). All rights reserved.

Sing a Song of Christmas — 4

†"Good Christian Men, Rejoice." Words Medieval Latin Carol. Music German Melody. Arrangement © copyright 1999 Van Ness Press, Inc. (ASCAP). All rights reserved.

†"Go, Tell It on the Mountain." Words by JOHN W. WORK, JR. Music African-American Spiritual.
Arrangement © copyright 1999 Van Ness Press, Inc. (ASCAP). All rights reserved.
††"Let Your Gladness Know No End." Words Traditional English. Music Old Bohemian Carol.
Arrangement © copyright 1999 Van Ness Press, Inc. (ASCAP). All rights reserved.

Sing a Song of Christmas — 8

Service Idea

CHRISTMAS CONCERT

Follow this suggested listing or determine the number of songs that will fit the time frame of your concert. Scripture passages may be chosen from the Celebration of Advent Service Idea (p. 206) and inserted to tell the Christmas story.

Openers:
"Jingle Bells Medley"
"Christmastime"
"Sing a Song of Christmas"

The Story:
"I Wonder as I Wander"
"O Magnify"
"Born in Bethlehem"
"Come, Let Us Go unto Bethlehem"
"Hark! The Herald Angels Sing"
"How Great Our Joy"
"Sing Noel"

Wrap-up:
"Once and for All"
"From the Cradle to the Cross"
"Because of Bethlehem"

Invitation:
"Come to My Heart, Lord Jesus"
"Light of the World"

Finale:
"Like Christmas All Year 'Round"
"Sing a Song of Christmas"
"Joy to the World! The Lord Is Come"

Service Idea

CELEBRATION OF ADVENT

Advent is the celebration of the Christmas story that traditionally begins four Sundays before Christmas. There are no specific guidelines for this celebration, although most involve lighting candles of an Advent wreath. A typical celebration also involves Scripture readings and songs appropriate to the story. Below is an Advent celebration incorporating the arrangements in *20/20: A Christmas Collection*.

WEEK 1

Narrator: The prophecy of the Baby is given.
(Isaiah 7:14; 9:6-7; Micah 5:2)

Choir: "Because of Bethlehem"

Congregation: "Come, Thou Long-Expected Jesus"
"O Come, O Come, Emmanuel"
"Lo, How a Rose E'er Blooming"

Choir: "I Wonder as I Wander"
"Joy to the World! The Lord Is Come"
"Come to My Heart, Lord Jesus"
"O Come, All Ye Faithful"

WEEK 2

Narrator: The Baby is born.
(Luke 1:26-38,46-48)

Choir: "O Magnify"

Narrator: Luke 2:1-7

Choir: "Sing Noel"
"Born in Bethlehem"
"Sing a Song of Christmas"

Congregation: "Silent Night, Holy Night"
"O Little Town of Bethlehem"
"The First Nowell"
"What Child Is This"
"The Birthday of a King"
"Away in a Manger"

WEEK 3

Narrator: The Baby is worshiped.
(Luke 2:8-20; Matthew 2:1-12)

Choir: "Hark! The Herald Angels Sing"
"Come, Let Us Go unto Bethlehem"
"Angels We Have Heard on High"
"O Come, All Ye Faithful"
"How Great Our Joy"

Congregation: Any of the carols from previous weeks
"Angels, from the Realms of Glory"
"O Holy Night"
"While Shepherds Watched Their Flocks"
"We Three Kings of Orient Are"

WEEK 4

Narrator: The baby Jesus is the Messiah.
(John 1:14; 3:16)

Choir: "From the Cradle to the Cross"
"I Wonder as I Wander"
"Once and for All"
"Because of Bethlehem"
"Light of the World"
"Come to My Heart, Lord Jesus"

Congregation: "O Come, Let Us Adore Him"
Any Christmas carol from previous weeks.

Service Idea

CHRISTMAS EVE SERVICE

Choral Call to Worship:	"Sing a Song of Christmas"
(optional)	"Christmastime"
Congregation:	"O Come, All Ye Faithful"
	"O Little Town of Bethlehem"
Narrator:	Luke 1:26-38,46-48
Choir:	"O Magnify"
	"I Wonder as I Wander"
	"Come, Let Us Go unto Bethlehem"
Narrator:	Luke 2:8-20; Matthew 2:1-12
Congregation:	"Angels, from the Realms of Glory"
	"O Holy Night"
Choir:	"Angels We Have Heard on High"
	"Come to My Heart, Lord Jesus"
	"How Great Our Joy"
Congregation/Choir:	"Joy to the World! The Lord Is Come"
Choir:	"Because of Bethlehem"
	"Light of the World"
	"From the Cradle to the Cross"
Congregation/Choir:	"Hark! The Herald Angels Sing"
	"O Come, All Ye Faithful"
Congregational candlelighting:	"Silent Night, Holy Night"
(optional)	
Choir:	"Sing Noel"
	"Christmastime"